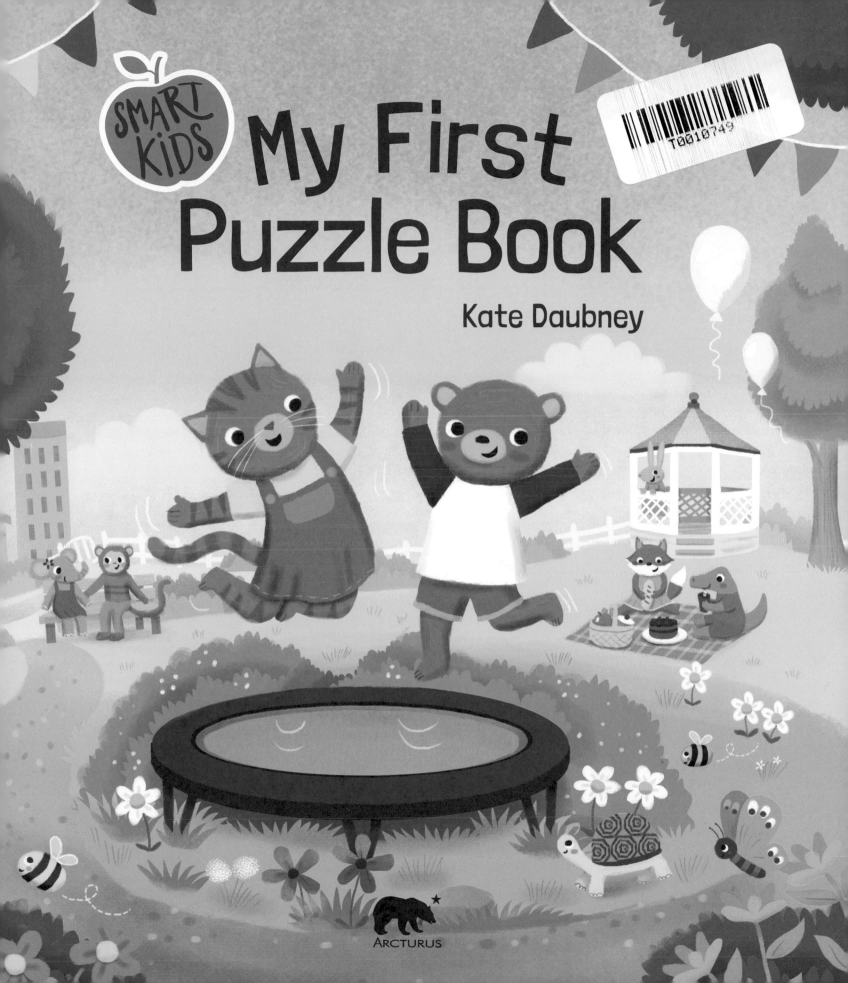

SMART KIDS
My First Puzzle Book

Kate Daubney

ARCTURUS

ARCTURUS

This edition published in 2023 by Arcturus Publishing Limited
26/27 Bickels Yard, 151–153 Bermondsey Street,
London SE1 3HA

Author: Harper Stewart
Illustrator: Kate Daubney
Editor: Violet Peto
Designer: Nathan Balsom
Managing Editor: Joe Harris
Design Manager: Jessica Holliland

ISBN: 978-1-3988-2582-6
CH010453NT
Supplier 29, Date 0523, PI 00003235

Printed in China

Robots

All of these toy robots look identical—apart from one. Can you spot it?

Ripe for the Picking

Ravi Racoon is gathering pears, and Geraldine Giraffe is gathering peaches. Who gets to gather the most fruit?

Time for Cake!

Kayla Koala is making a cake for Mrs. Hop's birthday! Help her finish the pattern of decorations on each tier by filling in the spaces.

Tasty Treats

Luna Lemur is collecting seashells at the beach. Can you spot the only seashell that does not have an identical match?

As Fast as a Fox

Finn is lost in the park!
Can you help him find his way out?

Crazy About Books

How many red books can you find in this library scene?

Ready, Set, Go!

The bike race is complete! Trace each route from top to bottom of the map, then match the flags to each competitor to decide who took the shortest route.

Talent Show

This talented trio have won first prize!
Can you spot seven differences between these two pictures?

Roll Up! Roll Up!

Look at those acrobats go! Can you find all the items from the panel on the right in this scene?

Find the Fish

All of these fish are different, apart from a pair of twins. Can you spot the two that look the same?

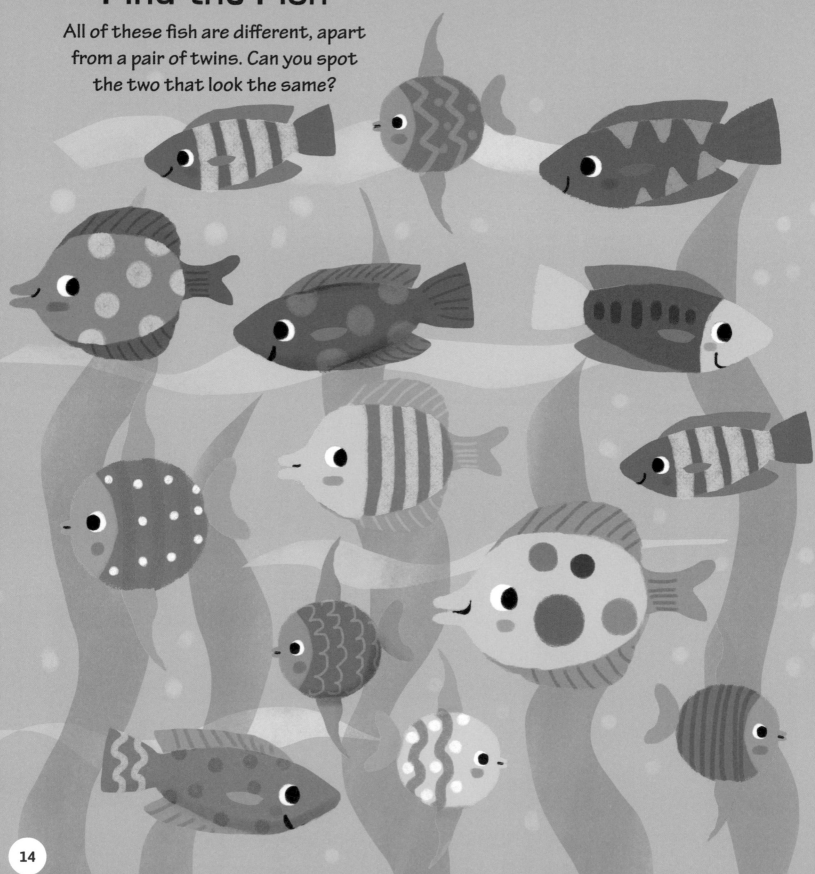

Turtley Confused

Tony Turtle lives on the log in the middle of the lake, but he can't seem to remember the way home! Can you help him choose the correct route to get there?

START

FINISH

Pretty as a Picture

Which three pieces are needed to complete the jigsaw puzzle of the Bear family portrait?

A

B

C

D

E

Eye of Newt

Help Merlin complete his magical mixture by following the potion order shown. You may move up, down, left, and right, but not diagonally.

START

FINISH

Strawberry Patch

It's a lovely day in the strawberry patch. How many strawberries can you find in this scene?

Beautiful Birds

Find the pairs of these pretty birds, and use pens or crayons to make the black-and-white one match its partner.

Spring Cleaning

Mrs. Hop needs your help to organize her beach shed.
Can you complete the pattern on each shelf by filling in the missing
items in the gaps?

Cloud Cover

Which three pieces are needed to finish this jigsaw puzzle?

A   B   C   D   E

Lunchtime!

Which of the construction workers is having a sandwich for lunch today? Follow the trails to find out!

Ahoy!

Match each pirate to their ship. Use the ships' sails to help you.

Kites

These kites look lovely up in the sky—but the last one needs finishing!
Follow the sequence, and decorate the blank kite using your pens and pencils.

Counting with Canoes

Which of the three canoes has the most passengers?

Party Time!

It's Mrs. Hop's birthday party!
Study the scene, and then decide whether
each of the sentences below is true or false.

- Kayla Koala and Herman Hippo are holding the banner.
- Everyone is wearing a party hat.
- Bruno Bear is wearing red shoes.
- Mabel Mouse is dancing.
- There are seven slices of cake.

Happy Birthday, Mrs. Hop!

Busy Bus

The bus is crowded today! Can you find all the items
from the panel on the right in this scene?

Sparkle and Shine

Each of these necklaces has a twin. Can you spot the one necklace that does not have an identical match?

Eat Up!

What a tasty meal Rasheed Rooster has prepared! Study this photo, then turn the page to see which of the items have swapped places.

Eat Up!

Can you figure out which of the items have swapped places?

Shoe Shenanigans

Patrick Porcupine has lost his other shoe!
Can you help him find it?

Creating Cupcakes

What delicious treats! Find each pair of cupcakes, and use pens or crayons to make the black-and-white one match its partner.

Mighty Mountain

Which three pieces are needed
to complete the jigsaw puzzle?

A   B   C   D   E

Marsh Maze

This duck is looking for his mother.
Can you help him find her?

START

FINISH

Inching Along

Help this hungry caterpillar munch his way through the forest by following the leaf pattern. You may move up, down, left, and right, but not diagonally.

Watch Them Twirl!

Which of the tiles isn't part of the main picture?

A

B

C

D

Busy Bee

Connect the dots to give the bees a home!
Can you guess what Tara Tiger is collecting?

10 11
9 12
8 13
7 14
6 15
5 1
4
3
2

Movie Night!

Can you spot six differences between
these two scenes?

Perfect Pizza

Which silhouette matches the picture of Masato Macaque?

Band Practice

Practice makes perfect! Study this picture of the orchestra,
then turn the page to see who has swapped places.

Band Practice

Can you figure out who has swapped places?

Pretty in Pink

Fernanda loves to show off her bright pink feathers! Can you find the word PINK hidden just once in the grid?

P	N	I	I	N	K	I	P
I	I	N	K	P	N	I	K	P
K	K	P	N	P	I	N	P	I
N	N	I	P	K	P	N	P	N
N	N	P	K	I	K	P	I	N
P	P	I	K	N	P	I	N	K
K	K	N	N	I	I	K	P	P
K	K	I	I	P	P	N	K	I

45

Flying High

See if you can find all of these beautiful balloons:

- A balloon being piloted by a penguin
- A pair of matching balloons
- A red, white, and yellow balloon

Butterflies

Find each pair of matching butterflies, and use pens or crayons to make each black-and-white one match its partner.

Enchanted Kingdom

Can you find all of the items shown in the panel on the right in this scene?

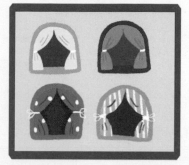

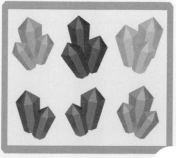

Catch of the Day

Owen Owl loves to fish! Can you help him get to the perfect fishing spot?

START

FINISH

Travel Bug

Look at all the cool places Kayla Koala has visited! Study the framed photos, then decide whether each of the sentences below is true or false.

- Kayla has never been to a city.
- The cottage she visited was white and blue.
- Kayla has never seen snow.
- Kayla is in all of the pictures.
- In one of the pictures, Kayla is wearing a pink dress.

Jungle Jigsaw

Which three pieces are needed to complete this jigsaw puzzle?

A

B

C

D

E

Breakfast Time

All of these loaves of bread look identical, apart from one. Can you spot it?

Splish–Splash!

Which of the tiles isn't part of the main picture?

High and Dry

Sunita is hanging up her washing.
Can you help her complete the pattern?
Which remaining clothes should she hang up
and where should they go?

A Lovely Lunch

Time for a picnic! The names of three types of food
are hidden in these letters. Can you find them?
Cross out all of the other letters.

JHKSANDWICHKJHSALADLHLIUPASTAHD

Sunday Outing

What a lovely summer's day! Connect the dots to reveal the rest of this hovering insect.

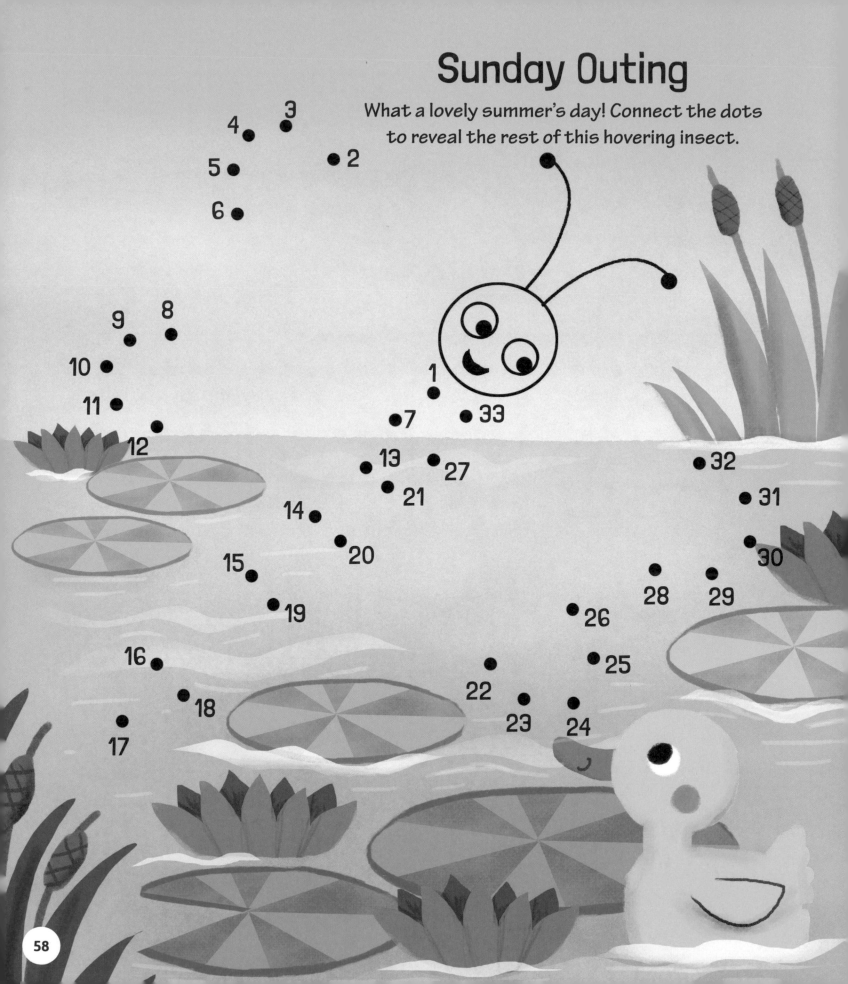

Dinnertime!

Paolo Panda is enjoying a plate of pasta!
Can you find the silhouette that matches the main picture?

Brush, Brush, Brush!

Jerome Jaguar wants you to remember to take care of your teeth! Can you find the word BRUSH hidden just once in the grid?

S	H	R	U	B	R	U	B
R	U	S	H	S	H	B	R
U	R	R	B	U	H	S	R
S	H	U	R	B	H	S	U
B	R	B	R	U	S	H	R
U	S	H	R	U	B	S	H
B	U	S	H	B	U	R	S
S	H	U	R	B	R	H	B

It's a Jungle out There!

Study this jungle scene, then turn the
page to see which of the animals have moved.

It's a Jungle out There!

Can you figure out which animals have moved?

It's a Mouthful

Which pelican has caught the most fish?

Hats Off!

All of these hats are different, apart from a matching pair.
Can you spot the two that look the same?

Creative Creations!

Pablo Pigasso's students are amazing artists!
Can you complete the pattern of artworks on each line?

Soaring Through the Sky

Connect the dots to reveal this beautiful hovering bird.
Use your pens and crayons to add bright shades.

Shell Seekers

What pretty shells! Study the shoreline below, then decide whether each of the sentences is true or false.

- All the shells are unique.
- There are four pink shells.
- The blue shell is bigger than the green shell.
- There is a hermit crab inside the yellow shell.
- There are eight shells in total.

Tennis Team

Write the names above or below each team member using the clues.

- Geraldine is wearing a bandana.
- Fatima has the biggest ears.
- The goat is named Gallia.
- Peter has spots.
- Bobby is black and white.
- Sunita is next to Bobby and Fatima.

Hustle and Bustle

Can you find all these items
in the busy train station?

- A red suitcase
- A cat napping
- An elephant wearing a hat

Bowled Over

Can you help Missy find her lucky bowling ball?

- It is patterned.
- It contains yellow but not green.

It's Chilly Out Here!

Can you match these penguins to their eggs?

Get Creative!

Brighten up this image using your pens and pencils!

Stargazers

Look at the beautiful night sky! Can you spot six differences between these two pictures?

Raining Cats and Dogs

Use your pens and pencils to finish
the sequence of umbrellas.

Garden Delights

Can you find the names of three flowers hidden in these letters?
Cross out the other letters.

BHROSENXFTVIOLETLPNDAISYHQU

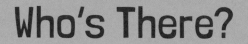

Who's There?

All of these sneaky spies are different,
apart from two in the same disguise.
Can you spot the matching pair?

High Up

Which climber will reach the top using the shortest route?

Off Your Rocker

One of these rocking horses is a tiny bit different. Which one is it?

Howdy There!

Study this picture, then turn the page to answer some questions about the scene.

Howdy There!

What can you remember without looking back?

- Was Panda's horse black or brown?

- How many snakes were there?

- Were the flowers on the cacti yellow or purple?

Ball Pit

How many of each ball can you spot in the ball pit?

In a Flurry

Who has won the ice sculpture competition?
Follow the clues to find out!
The winner is wearing the items listed in the yellow box.

- A hat
- Black boots
- A patterned scarf

Flower Power

Find a pair to each pretty vase, then use your pens and pencils to make the black-and-white one match its partner.

Answers

Page 3

Page 4

There are 7 pears and 9 peaches, so Geraldine Giraffe gets to gather the most fruit.

Page 5

Page 6

Page 7

Pages 8–9

There are six red books.

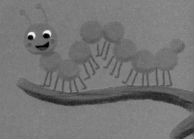

Page 10

The pig took the
shortest route
to the finish line.

Page 11

Pages 12–13

Page 14

Page 15

Page 16

Page 17

Pages 18–19

There are eight strawberries.

Page 20

Page 21

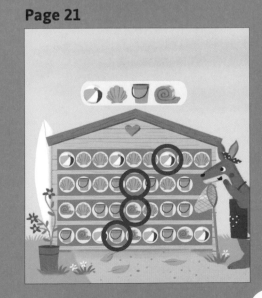

Page 22

Page 23

Page 24

Page 25

Page 26

Page 27

- Kayla Koala and Herman Hippo are holding the banner. TRUE

- Everyone is wearing a party hat. FALSE—the fox is not wearing a party hat

- Bruno Bear is wearing red shoes. FALSE—Bruno Bear is wearing blue shoes.

- Mabel Mouse is dancing. TRUE

- There are seven slices of cake. FALSE—There are nine slices of cake.

Pages 28–29

Page 30

Pages 31–32

These items have swapped places: the salad and the cup.

Page 33

Page 34

Page 35

Page 36

Page 37

Pages 38–39

Page 40

Tara Tiger is collecting honey from a bees' nest!

Page 41

Page 42

90

Pages 43–44

These orchestra members have swapped places: Panda and Cat; Crocodile and Flamingo.

Page 45

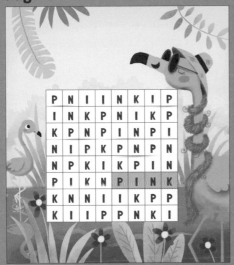

Page 46

● A balloon being piloted by a penguin

● A pair of matching balloons

● A red, white, and yellow balloon

Page 47

Pages 48–49

Page 50

Page 51

Kayla has never been to a city. FALSE

The cottage she visited was white and blue. TRUE

Kayla has never seen snow. FALSE

Kayla is in all of the pictures. FALSE

In one of the pictures, Kayla is wearing a pink dress. TRUE

Page 52

Page 53

Pages 54–55

Page 56

Page 57

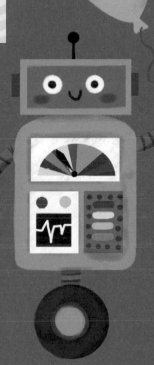

Page 58

Page 59

Page 60

S	H	R	U	B	R	U	B
R	U	S	H	S	H	B	R
U	R	R	B	U	H	S	R
S	H	U	R	B	H	S	U
B	R	**B**	**R**	**U**	**S**	**H**	R
U	S	H	R	U	B	S	H
B	U	S	H	B	U	R	S
S	H	U	R	B	R	H	B

Pages 61–62

These animals have swapped places: the toucan and the frog; the purple bird and the butterfly.

Page 63

10 fish

11 fish

Page 64

Page 65

Page 66

Page 67

- All the shells are unique. TRUE

- There are four pink shells. TRUE

- The blue shell is bigger than the green shell. TRUE

- There is a hermit crab inside the yellow shell. FALSE—there is a hermit crab inside the purple shell.

- There are eight shells in total. TRUE

Page 68

BOBBY SUNITA FATIMA

GERALDINE GALLIA PETER

Page 69

- A red suitcase
- A cat having a nap
- An elephant wearing a hat

Page 70

Page 71

Page 73

Page 74

Page 75

Page 76

Page 77

The racoon used the shortest route to the finish.

Page 78

Page 80

Panda's horse was brown.

There were two snakes.

The flowers on the cacti were purple.

Page 81

5   3   7   8

Page 82

The porcupine won the ice sculpture competition.

Page 83